Guide to Good Manners

From Precious Parents
to Precious Kids

by Joelle Richa

Hatherleigh Press is committed to preserving and protecting the natural resources of the earth. Environmentally responsible and sustainable practices are embraced within the company's mission statement.

Visit us at www.hatherleighpress.com and register online for free offers, discounts, special events, and more.

Guide to Good Manners
Copyright © 2015 Joelle Richa

Library of Congress Cataloging-in-Publication Data is available upon request.
ISBN: 978-1-57826-580-0

Printed in Canada
10 9 8 7 6 5 4 3 2 1

Guide to Good Manners

From Precious Parents to Precious Kids

the journey to learn good manners

Etiquette starts at home and expands to the outside world. So respond to your parents' desire to teach you good manners. You will be their pride and joy.

Dear Parents,

Courtesy begins at home. This book is designed to be your companion in the journey of teaching your kids how to adopt and practice good manners. Your beloved children will appreciate your efforts and be forever grateful.

Your children are the treasures of your life. Equip them with etiquette and precious principles of good manners for the endearment of their lives. Read this guide with your children with enjoyment and wisdom, and you will be rewarded after inspiring them to acquire pleasant and polite attitudes in society. Practicing good manners in public will project your children into the center of attention and praises.

Give them incentives in return for learning etiquette at a young age. You will be proud and receive amiable remarks from neighbors, relatives, friends, and teachers concerning their excellent behavior. Spend a few moments with them every day to teach and acknowledge polite attitudes. The result will exceed all of your expectations.

Good luck in this remarkable task; it will brighten up your days.

⚜

SPECIAL THANKS
Gretchen Best
Debbie Moseson
And my family:
Joseph, Nany, Sandrine and Laurence and Brian Purdin

Don't be a liar. Tell the truth, even when you did wrong, and apologize.

INSIDE-OUTSIDE WITH OTHERS

This section outlines the preferred behavior of children as they relate to others both inside and outside their homes.

Inside your community, your school, or with friends, always show respect and kindness toward others.

Always respect others, no matter what their disposition. Everyone has a unique appearance and personality. Admire all the flavors of your community and the world.

Be compassionate and understanding about differences of race, color, and origins.

Shake hands when you meet a friend or a new acquaintance. Don't be shy to do it.

Give a kiss or a hug to a fellow recovering from illness or accident, and wish them an excellent recovery.

Be on time for the school bus, an appointment, a sports game, theater performance, or other event.

When you play with others, manage and protect their toys and belongings as you would your own.

Don't be a liar. Tell the truth, even when you do wrong, and apologize.

At the pool, avoid shouting, screaming, or pushing kids in the water.

While at the pool, respect the swimmer's relaxation and tranquility.

Show restraint and don't panic when a fire alarm goes off. Help others to locate the exit door.

Always look for a trash can to throw away your waste.

Learn to share. If you play a game on the computer, give others the opportunity to enjoy a period to play also. You can't monopolize the computer for yourself.

Don't make fun of your brother or sister while you are in company. Discrediting him or her does not make you a valued person. On the contrary, it reduces your credibility.

Prevent your siblings from being aggressive toward others. Comfort the victim and make peace.

Show your commitment to being fair and impartial in any argument or quarrel between friends.

Avoid yelling or shouting in hallways, stairs, or elevators.

Keep your music at a decent volume. Don't disrupt the business of others.

Close a door slowly. Don't slam or bang an entrance or internal door.

Offer help to an elderly person with bags, and open the doors for him or her.

Never interrupt a conversation.
Just wait until it is finished to
state your question or remark.

When on a bus or metro, give away your seat to an elderly person, a pregnant woman, or a handicapped passenger.

Use the magic words "please", "thank you", "you are welcome", "excuse me", "I beg your pardon", or "I am sorry" each time you confront a situation. They define your degree of politeness.

Address a lady by "madam" or "misses" and a gentleman by "sir" or "mister."

Be the first to salute by saying "good morning, madam" or "sir" when you meet someone.

Never interrupt a conversation. Just wait until it is finished to state your question or remark.

Don't rush to the school bus or jump in a cafeteria line by pushing others.

Use your hand to cover your mouth when you sneeze, cough, or yawn.

Prevent making noises when your parents are sleeping. Your effort to be silent will be appreciated.

Avoid playing or waving your arms with food in your hands. You can easily soil your or a friend's clothes.

Never talk when chewing. Keep your mouth closed and chew silently.

Don't spit in the street or other public places. It is disgraceful to spit in public.

Never talk when chewing. Keep your mouth closed and chew silently.

Raise your hand and wait for teachers to allow you to answer.

Introduce your friend or companion when you meet somebody.

Never laugh at the misfortune of anyone who stumbles; instead, rush to offer help.

Respect your grandparents; they love to feel your affection and your care.

Listen to your teacher with attention and concentration, instead of talking or disturbing your classmates.

Raise your hand and wait for the teacher to allow you to answer or ask a question.

Do not use bad words when you are angry or frustrated. Never lose your self-control. You will be respected for restraining your emotions.

Boys: Let a girl be served first. It is a gallant gesture, and the girls will love it!

Don't point a finger at anyone—ever!

Be a good loser; and play fair. Don't display a bad temper, but instead congratulate the winner. You will make a superb impression.

Don't be curious by trying to listen to another conversation. It is not a polite attitude. Respect the privacy of people sitting close to you.

Avoid burping in public or at the dinner table. If it happens, say "Excuse me. I am sorry."

When you play with others, manage and protect their toys and belongings as you would your own.

Don't stick your gum under a chair, seat, or table. Keep it in a paper tissue and wait to find a trash can.

It is rude, dirty, and unhealthy to clean your teeth with your fingernail. If you are in public, go to the restroom and clean your teeth with a toothpick. At home, excuse yourself to brush your teeth in the bathroom.

Never "play" in your nose. It is disgusting and repulsive.

Don't wipe your nose at the dinner table. Excuse yourself from the area to do it in the bathroom.

Tidy up your room. You will provide relief to your parents. Keeping your room in order is a reflection of your personality. Your friends will love to visit you and spend time in your clean room.

Ask your parents for permission if you plan to invite a friend to your house.

If you sleep at a friend's house, be respectful and preserve whatever you touch or play with so you will be invited frequently.

Don't forget to present a small gift when you are invited. It is an elegant and thoughtful gesture.

Don't continue watching television or surfing the internet when you have a visitor.

Check your
school bag before
leaving home!

Never slander or gossip about someone in their absence.

Make your phone calls after 8 a.m. and before 10 p.m. Answer politely and avoid being rude if you receive a wrong call.

Don't speak loudly on a cell phone when you are on a bus, in a restaurant, or on the street. It is your private matter.

During a personal conversation, look in the person's eyes, speak softly, and use a clear voice.

Don't forget to set your alarm clock before you go to sleep at night.

Start your day with a good breakfast before leaving for school. It will help you to stay focused in the classroom.

Brush your teeth and put on clean clothes and shoes before you leave the house. Don't forget to make your bed!

Check your school bag before leaving home.

Kiss your parents before leaving for school.

Of course, you also don't want to forget to treat your pets before you depart for school!

Don't bust into a line.

offer help to an elderly person with bags and open the doors for him or her.

always respect others

Wish excellent recovery

Be on time . . . .

Prevent your siblings from being aggressive toward others--

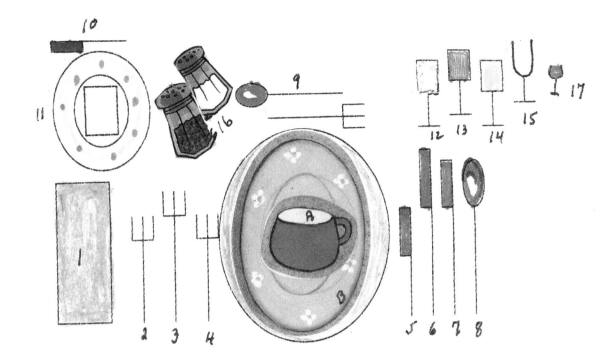

1 - napkin.
2 - Fish Fork.
3 - Dinner Fork
4 - Salad Fork.

A - Soupbowl + plate.
B - Dinner plate.

5 - Salad Knife.
6 - Dinner Knife.
7 - Fish Knife.
8 - Soup Spoon

10 - Butter Knife.
11 - Butter plate + Bread.

9 - Silverware dessert.

16 - Salt + pepper
      Shakers.

12 - Water glass.
13 - Wine glass (Red).
14 - Wine glass (white).
15 - Champagne flute.
17 - liquor glass.

AT THE DINNER TABLE

Take off your hat, wash your hands, and be respectful.

Listen with respect to the prayer said before you start eating your dinner.

Don't use your table chair as a rocking chair.

Don't play with silverware when waiting to be served.

Sit straight and don't hunch over your plate. Don't prop your head while you eat.

Don't place your wrists or forearms around your plate. If you need to wait, keep you hands on your lap.

Wait until everybody is seated and served to start eating.

The bread is always placed on your left and the water glass on your right.

Avoid being grumpy if you don't like the food.

Avoid being a sloppy eater. Do it with finesse and style.

Don't grab your fork or spoon. Hold it between the thumb, index finger, and middle finger (of your left hand).

With your right hand, hold your knife by the middle of the handle with your index finger on the top of it.

Don't gobble your food when you start eating and avoid gulping your drink.

Use your napkin to clean your fingers and mouth. Put your napkin back on your lap.

Eat with your mouth closed and avoid noisy chewing.

Never speak with your mouth full!

Take the bread with your fingers, not with a fork. Break it slowly by hand.

Never bring a knife to your mouth.

When you start with soup, don't blow on it if it is hot. Wait until it is cooler. You should tilt the soup plate away from you to get the last bit of soup.

Avoid being grumpy if you don't like the food.

While you are waiting to be served, show your appreciation for the food and the menu. Always compliment the one who prepared the meal.

Ask for salt, pepper, or butter. Don't try to extend your arm to reach them.

If you leave the table during the meal, place your napkin on your chair.

Hold the glass by its stem when you drink.

Eat eggs, cakes, or salads with the designated fork only. Do the same with pie.

Don't answer or use a cell phone at the dinner table.

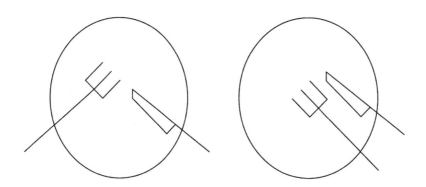

Before leaving the table, put the unfolded napkin beside your plate, and keep your fork and knife at the corner of your plate.

Thank your parents or your friend's parents after the meal, and ask permission to leave the table. Push in your chair.

Go directly to the bathroom to wash your hands and clean your teeth.

Ask for salt, pepper, or butter.
Don't try to extend your arm
to reach them.

Ask if you can help to clear the table.

Show your appreciation for the food to the host/hostess. You will be invited more often! "Thank you, madam. The food was excellent and delicious."

Use your napkin to clean fingers and mouth. Put your napkin back on your lap.

Never speak with your mouth full!

Ask if you can help to clear the table.

ABOUT HYGIENE

Wash your hands before eating a meal, leaving the library, surfing the internet, or finishing a book or magazine. Also, wash up after playing a game.

Keep your nails clean. It is essential to your health and your clean appearance.

It is important to take a shower after you sweat, especially after a sporting event. It prevents a bad odor. It is unpleasant for a girl or boy to have armpits or feet that smell.

Never use deodorant on sweaty armpits. The best option is to take a shower.

It is relaxing to take a shower before bedtime. Try to do it every night.

Clean hair defines your radiant image. Shiny, groomed hair provides a nice look. Always keep your hair in neat condition.

Your lovely smile depends on healthy and clean teeth. Don't eat candy before bedtime. Brush your teeth before sleep, when you wake up, and after every meal. It protects your teeth and keeps the dentist away.

Always look both ways before crossing the street.

Scratching your head or your lower body at the dinner table or in the living room with guests is disrespectful. Do it in a private area and wash your hands afterward.

It is ugly to bite one's nails. It is dirty and unhealthy. It shows a lack of self-control and confidence, and presents an off-putting image of your personality. Parents are asked to look at the problem with a psychologist's advice.

STREET BEHAVIOR

Walk on the right side of the sidewalk on your way to school.

If you overtake someone walking slowly, do it from their left side.

When you walk, look straight in front of you. Don't drop your head or you may run into another pedestrian.

While crossing the street at an intersection, thank the driver who stopped with a hand wave.

Cross at the red light, and use the lane designed for pedestrians.

Be attentive and keep your eyes on the traffic signal. Wait for the signal to cross.

Always look both ways before crossing the street.

Always hold the hand of an adult while crossing.

Never accept the proposition of a ride given by a stranger and try to memorize the plate number of the vehicle.

SECURITY MEASURES

Always keep your house phone number in your pocket.

Leave the phone number for your friend's house with your parents when you are invited to visit.

Indicate the time of your return home to your loved ones. If you are late, call to warn them.

Never accept the proposition of a stranger to give you a ride, and try to memorize the plate number of the vehicle.

Always use the same route from school or a friend's home. Make your parents aware of the itinerary.

Don't interrupt a face to face
conversation to answer a call.
You show that he or she is
un important to you.

WIRELESS MANNERS

The invention of the cell phone can bring people together and overcome barriers and distances, so use it with grace and good manners.

Don't use the cell phone to intrude on someone's privacy.

Be a nice caller, and keep your conversations short.

Finish your call, turn off the cell, and start a face-to-face conversation.

Politeness and cell phone use can co-exist, so use it for respectable purposes.

Don't yell when talking on a cell phone. Nobody wants to be privy to your personal conversations.

Excuse yourself before taking a call when you are with somebody.

Use the "vibrate" feature in the theater, library, church, meeting, or any other public gathering.

Don't interrupt a face-to-face conversation to answer a call. You show that he or she is unimportant to you.

Keep private matters private.

Don't text in a conference or meeting .....

Don't talk on the cell phone in restrooms, elevators, waiting rooms, auditoriums, buses, or trains.

Don't let your phone ring during a classroom session.

Don't let the cell ring at the dinner table. Leave it on the "vibrate" feature.

Respect personal space, and move away from people to answer the call.

Be polite and discreet when you speak.

Don't text when you are at the dinner table.

Gesturing in the street when you talk on the cell phone gives a crazy impression.

Don't text when you cross an intersection or when you ride a bike. This is dangerous to you and other pedestrians.

Don't text in a seminar or meeting.

Texting must not interrupt your homework. There is time for every activity, but your school obligations should always come first.

Sexting is illegal and can expose you to harsh problems and psychological damage.

Don't use texting to do harm to somebody. Politeness is a great rule in texting.

The Internet opens the world to you. Use it to enhance your knowledge, not for futile moments.

The Internet opens a window to make contacts with others. Respect differences of opinions and engage in dialogue about roots, history, color, language, and sport without a critical attitude.

The Internet helps you reach all frontiers. Be polite and respectful.

"The Internet helps you"
to reach all frontiers

Be motivated by an interest to learn, not to criticize others.

Resist any chat about vulgar subjects, and confine discussions to respectable matters.

Don't give your email address to a stranger. Limit the access to close friends and relatives. A credit card number must not be provided either.

Inform your parents about any suspicious person. Interrupt the conversation and switch to another contact rapidly.

Children must be aware of sex offenders who surf the Internet. Never engage in an intimate conversation with a stranger or accept any invitation to meet. Don't keep it a secret, and inform your parents.

Avoid indiscreetly sharing details about your family when you surf on a public chat site.

Keep only moral and upstanding citizens on your contact lists.

Don't argue about religion, faith, or beliefs with your online contacts.

When 'Trick or Treating' on Halloween,
always be polite and nice in
your community.

FOR KIDS TO REMEMBER

A smiling kid opens the windows of happiness.

Clean and shiny hair is a mark of self-esteem.

Always wear clean shoes or sneakers and appealing clothes.

Brush your teeth and keep fresh breath.

Keep your hands and nails clean.

Respectful attitudes and behavior are admired.

Don't use bad words in fury.

Making fun of a friend with health problems is disgraceful.

Show your humane side and your desire to help, support, or comfort others.

Respect and obey your teachers. They are the ones who prepare you for a bright future.

A gallant boy attracts the attention of nice girls.

A stylish girl is in the spotlight and will be admired by everyone.

Your homework is the reflection of your self-esteem, so do it properly.

Be a peacemaker at school, not a troublemaker.

Stay quiet on the school bus and respect the driver.

The Internet is a tool for knowledge, so don't use it for degrading purposes or inappropriate subjects.

Praise the Lord every day for having wonderful parents surrounding you with love and protection.

Bless your parents' efforts and sacrifices to provide you a good education. Be grateful and full of recognition.

Your home is your kingdom; keep it clean and tidy.

Be in full solidarity with your siblings. Show them love and joy.

Be proud of your parents and reward them with your excellent report cards.

REFLECTIONS

"You give but little when you give of your possessions. It is when you give of yourself that you truly give."

"And beauty is not a need but an ecstasy. It is not a mouth thirsting, nor an empty hand stretched forth, but rather a heart enflamed and a soul enchanted…Beauty is eternity gazing at itself in a mirror. But you are eternity and you are the mirror."

"And let your best be for your friend…
Seek him always with hours to live.
For it is his to fill your need, but not your emptiness.
And in the sweetness of friendship let there be laughter,
and sharing of pleasures.
For in the dew of little things, the heart finds its morning and is refreshed."

(From *The Prophet* by Kahlil Gibran)

IN CONCLUSION

It is never too early to start learning good manners, because when bad habits occur, it becomes too hard to get rid of them.

Etiquette starts at home and expands to the outside world, so respond to your parents' desire to teach you good manners. You will be their pride and joy.

Family is your treasure, solidarity is the cement, and love ties the bond between them.

For a boy: The aim of this book is to enhance your capacity to be a leader of tomorrow.

For a girl: The purpose of this book is to help you become a woman with a bright future.

For parents: "You are the bows from which your children as living arrows are sent forth. The archer sees the mark upon the path of the infinite, and He bends you with His might that His arrows may go swift and far. Let your bending in the archer's hand be for gladness; For even as He loves the arrow that flies, so He loves also the bow that is stable." (From *The Prophet* by Kahlil Gibran)